LIVING IN SIN?

A STUDY GUIDE FOR INDIVIDUALS AND SMALL GROUPS

Living in Sin?

A BISHOP RETHINKS HUMAN SEXUALITY

John Shelby Spong

**A STUDY GUIDE FOR INDIVIDUALS AND SMALL GROUPS
BY JUDITH L. HEGG**

HarperSanFrancisco
A Division of HarperCollins*Publishers*

LIVING IN SIN?: *A Study Guide for Individuals and Small Groups.* Copyright ©
1995 by HarperCollins. All rights reserved. Printed in the United States of
America. No part of this book may be used or reproduced in any manner
whatsoever without written permission except in the case of brief quotations
embodied in critical articles and reviews. For information address
HarperCollins Publishers, 10 East 53rd Street, New York, NY 10022.

FIRST EDITION

Study Guide ISBN 0–06–067551–9 (pbk)

Library of Congress Cataloging-in-Publication Data
Spong, John Shelby.
Living in Sin? : a bishop rethinks human sexuality / John Shelby Spong.
p.   cm.
Bibliography: p.
Includes index.
ISBN 0–06–067505-5 (alk. paper)
1. Sex—Religious aspects—Christianity.   I. Title
BT708.S66 1988
261.8'357—dc20   87–33654
                                                                          CIP

95   96   97   98   ❖   DICK   10   9   8   7   6   5   4   3   2   1

This edition is printed on acid-free paper that meets the American National
Standards Institute Z39.48 Standard.

CONTENTS

PROFILE OF THE RIGHT REVEREND
JOHN SHELBY SPONG

John Shelby Spong, author of fourteen books and more than seventy published articles, is a bishop in the Episcopal Church. His writings and extensive media appearances have made him a household name in his own denomination and a sought-after lecturer and guest speaker in Protestant circles on several continents as well as in some Roman Catholic communities.

Bishop Spong was born in 1931 in Charlotte, North Carolina, and was educated in the public schools of that city. He graduated Phi Beta Kappa in 1952 from the University of North Carolina at Chapel Hill and received his Master of Divinity degree in 1955 from the Protestant Episcopal Theological Seminary in Virginia. Both that seminary and St. Paul's College have conferred on him honorary Doctor of Divinity degrees. He served as rector of two parishes in North Carolina between 1955 and 1965, and two parishes in Virginia from 1965 to 1976. In 1976 he was consecrated bishop coadjutor of the Diocese of Newark and became the diocesan bishop in 1979.

The bishop speaks openly of his love for the holy Scriptures, which he traces to a Christmas gift of a Bible that he received as a young boy. Early daily reading of this book and later study and research laid the foundation for his interest in Christian education. All his southern pastorates as well as his episcopate have had as their hallmarks his crusade for high-quality adult Christian education. His willingness to discuss his views in high-profile situations has led to national television coverage of debates with noted biblical conservatives such as Jerry Falwell and Episcopal bishop William Wantland as well as a videotaping with Anglican author and scholar John R. W. Stott of London.

Unafraid to sail into uncharted waters, Bishop Spong has seen many of his books and other writings unleash wild storms of protest and outrage. Even *Living in Sin?* was born in controversy. Scheduled for publication by Abingdon Press, the denominational publisher of the United Methodist Church, the book was canceled three weeks before its release date as potentially too divisive. Picked up by Harper & Row and brought to publication just before the Episcopal church's 1988 general convention, which would be discussing whether practicing homosexuals should be ordained, the book became an immediate best-seller. Within weeks, Bishop Spong had been interviewed on fifteen television programs, five of them on national networks, and twenty-one radio shows.

Bishop Spong continues to be seen on national television as his views on the biblical birth narratives, the resurrection, the literal understanding of the Bible, and issues of sexuality are debated in the public arena. He challenges the Church's traditional standards in both his writings and his lectures, bringing many persons long ignored by the Church back into its fold. The dialogue he has initiated continues.

He says about *Living in Sin?*, "I do recognize that some people will be dislocated and angry but that response, I believe, will finally give way as the search for truth moves on. I feel confident that some ten to twenty-five years from now my position as I have presented it in this book will be normative in the church. For I am convinced that what I have written and the debate I have helped to launch will ultimately serve that Lord who, according to the fourth gospel, said not just to the righteous but presumably to all people, 'I have come that you might have life and have it more abundantly.'"*

---

* Taken from "At the Heart of the Matter," by John Shelby Spong, in *Books and Religion*, Spring–Summer 1989, pp. 13, 18.

PURPOSE OF THE STUDY GUIDE

Living in Sin? A Bishop Rethinks Human Sexuality is nothing if not provocative, and Bishop Spong fully intended the book to open debate on the issues he raises. Therefore, the Study Guide is designed first to assist you, the reader, in understanding the author's major points and supportive documentation. A second and equally important purpose, however, is to encourage you to articulate your own feelings and arguments about the many issues the bishop has raised. These two goals are accomplished primarily by incorporating five activities into the reading of the individual chapters: (1) the reading of a summary of a specific section or chapter; (2) the reading of biblical passages noted by the author as applicable to these pages; (3) the documenting of new insights that specific chapters and their accompanying biblical material have generated for you; (4) the answering of discussion questions; and (5) the recording in a journal or notebook the personal feelings that have been engendered. The journal, particularly, is expected to be an integral part of the process as you isolate your own feelings, prejudices, and concerns.

DIRECTIONS FOR USING THE STUDY GUIDE

As you begin your study of *Living in Sin?* you will need to assemble a few materials in addition to the book and the Study Guide. First, you should have a copy of either the Revised Standard Version (RSV) of the Bible or the New Revised Standard Version (NRSV). If you are especially comfortable with another edition, you are urged to use that *in addition to* one of the other two. Second, you will be directed to write in a journal at regular intervals. This journal can be either a loose-leaf notebook or a hardbound book of blank pages. Whatever you select should have a sense of permanence—it should not be a tablet of loose pages, for example—since you will be encouraged to reread your entries. Third, you should bring an open mind to the admittedly controversial material in this book. Obviously this is not an easy task, but growth and change come from entertaining new and challenging ideas. It may be that you will find your earlier beliefs strengthened, but they may be modified or perhaps reversed. As you begin your reading, be open to new ideas as they come to you. Do not be afraid to take them in previously unexplored directions; on the other hand, continue to challenge them with your own experience and reasoning.

The Study Guide format of each portion of the book will be similar.

1. Begin each study section by reading the appropriate chapter or chapters in *Living in Sin?* Following this you will be directed to read the summary or digest of the material in the Study Guide.

2. In most of the chapters Bishop Spong suggests biblical readings that support his arguments. If this is the case, you should at this point locate the biblical references in his writing and find and read them in the Bible you have available. While you are reading them, ask yourself why the author included this reference and if you believe it effectively supports his thesis.

A note about biblical notation: The first number after the name of the Bible book identifies the chapter that is cited; the numbers after the colon are the verses. Therefore, Mark 2 would indicate the entire second chapter of Mark; Mark 2:14 would designate the second chapter of Mark, verse 14; and Mark 2:14–16 would be the second chapter of Mark, verses

14 through 16. Some of the books have similar names—differentiated only by their beginning numerals—such as 1 Chronicles and 2 Chronicles. Be certain you are reading the appropriate reference.

3. There follows an opportunity for you to write in the Study Guide any new insights acquired while reading the chapter and the biblical references. These insights might include, for example, a new awareness or understanding, a new fact, a new connection, an intriguing image, or a fresh discovery.

4. Next, you will be asked to read, think about, and answer the question for reflection in order to look beyond Bishop Spong's words and examples. If you are using the Study Guide alone, it is suggested that you write out your answers to these discussion or reflection questions. However, if you are proceeding through the material with another person or several people, discuss these questions with them. Working together will encourage and stimulate further ideas about the material.

5. The final step for each chapter is writing in your journal. Your focus for this recording should be on concerns, unanswered questions, and personal feelings about the portion of the material just completed. The purpose of this activity is to encourage you to articulate how the reading has engaged you. Bishop Spong has anticipated that some of his ideas may surprise or shock you, but some may confuse you. And, of course, like many other people, you may encounter the pain of discovering personal prejudices of which you were unaware. When you have finished the book and the Study Guide, you will have in your journal a collection of personal concerns and feelings that the book has evoked. You will certainly know more about Bishop Spong and his theology, but you will also know more about yourself and how you react to ideas that challenge your formerly untested convictions or your personal prejudices and biases. Even if you are working with a small group in your study of *Living in Sin?*, it is important that each person keep his or her own journal.

FORMAT OF CHAPTERS IN THE STUDY GUIDE

Because of the manner in which the author has presented the material in the book, not all Study Guide sections will be the same length, and some portions will have longer summaries and more discussion questions. Further, some chapters have more biblical references than others and will therefore take longer for you to complete. In an effort to equalize the sections as much as possible, some chapters of the book have been combined into one Study Guide section. In one instance, chapter 7, the material has been divided into two Study Guide sections.

READY TO BEGIN

At this point, it is suggested that you open your journal and commence your work by recording a list of your expectations in reading *Living in Sin?* and the accompanying Study Guide. You will refer to this list when you have finished the book to determine if your goals have been met. Begin now by reading the preface to *Living in Sin?*

PART I

The Revolution

SETTING THE STAGE

and

A BIBLICAL CALL TO INCLUSIVENESS

SUMMARY

The houselights dim, the audience hushes expectantly, and a man—a bishop—walks to the center of the stage as the lights brighten. We are about to hear from the author of this work, *Living in Sin?*, his understanding of the call of Christians and by extension the call of the Christian church. In these first two chapters, Spong prepares the reader for the material that lies ahead.

This is a book about sex, yes, but less about sex than about prejudice and the fear that follows that prejudice. As individuals we often choose to reject and ultimately condemn things that we do not understand or that differ markedly from our own lifestyle and beliefs. The result is likely to be not only anger but also violence against those who hold these different views. Unfortunately, we suspend reason and dismiss new ideas. Our minds have snapped shut.

But the world is awash with new information about human sexuality, and we are called to examine these data, to suspend our judgments for a period, and to enter openly into debate. Because the Bible is a major resource for our decision making, the author plans, in the pages that follow, to look deeply at the place of Scripture in this dialogue.

God's call for the church is to be a "community for all people." Thus, we should see in this church community as diverse a people as we see in the population as a whole. Unfortunately, it is immensely easier to agree in word to this inclusivity than it is to live it, because, in the end, our prejudice gets in the way.

This intolerance and prejudice is not new to the twentieth century. Indeed, it can be seen in many places in the Bible itself. In an artful, humorous retelling of the story of Jonah, Spong reveals the prophetic response to this discrimination and bigotry: opposition to a narrow, exclusive faith that banishes those of whom we do not approve.

It is perhaps the fifth century B.C.E., and the Jewish people are seeking a reason for the defeat of their army and their subsequent life in captivity. Concluding that the cause of their plight is disobedience of God's law, they begin to root out from their midst all people whom they believe may have contaminated them with their presence: foreigners, non-Jewish spouses, all persons different from themselves. Into this charged atmosphere steps an unnamed prophet who tells a story—a story with a moral. This prophet urges his listeners to remember their mission: to preach to all persons of the all-encompassing nature of God's love. God's love is infinitely greater than their own, which has set up barriers and prejudiced restrictions.

This inclusivity is repeated in the New Testament in many places. See, for example, "In Christ shall *all* be made alive" (1 Cor. 15:22). Yet, throughout the history of the church, there have been threats to this call to inclusiveness. As early as the first century, the question of whether gentiles could become Christians was an issue. More recently, discrimination has existed against blacks, divorced persons who remarried, and individuals whose definition of sexual morality differed from that espoused by the church. The Old Testament message of Jonah is as timely today as it was twenty-five hundred years ago: God's love and acceptance exceed our own.

BIBLICAL READINGS

Deuteronomy 23:3	Matthew 28:19
Jonah 8	Romans 8:39
Matthew 11:28	1 Corinthians 15:22

NEW INSIGHTS

....

....

....

QUESTIONS FOR REFLECTION

1. What do you believe the word *proof-texting* (p. 25) means?

2. Bishop Spong claims that behind prejudice there is fear. Do you believe this? Why or why not? If you answered yes, what examples would you give to substantiate your claim?

3. If, as the author claims, the Bible itself is not free of contradictions and expressions of prejudice, of what value is this collection of books Christians call sacred Scripture?

4. Have you ever felt unwelcomed or rejected by the church or known anyone else who did? For what reasons? Do you believe that the church should accept *all* persons? Is no one to be excluded—ever?

5. Name some things about which you are absolutely certain. How did you come to your conclusions? Would you be willing to debate or dialogue with someone about your stand? What is your opinion of those who would not engage in such a discussion?

6. Give some examples of stories, like Jonah, that are powerful because they lead us to reflect on ourselves and our motives.

7. Have you ever heard this hymn that has often been sung to the tune of an old spiritual? What do you believe its message is? How would you change its words to correspond more closely to your beliefs about the Christian church?

In Christ there is no East or West,
in him no South or North,
But one great fellowship of love
throughout the whole wide earth.

Join hands, disciples of the faith,
whate'er your race may be!
Who serves my Father as his child
*is surely kin to me.**

*Words by John Oxenham (1852–1941)

ACTIVITY

Now begin writing in your journal. Take time to enter your feelings about the book so far. If you have unanswered questions, issues you wish the author had emphasized, or points of disagreement with the author, include those as well. This is your opportunity to dialogue with Bishop Spong.

CHAPTER THREE

THE SEXUAL REVOLUTION

SUMMARY

The twentieth century has been a time of enormous change as issues surrounding three interconnected movements work themselves out: women's issues, environmental concerns, and peace and disarmament issues. Underlying these three themes and at the heart of them is a shift in understanding of the proper balance between men and women in society.

A patriarchal foundation has shaped our history for thousands of years, but changes are in the air. In time, survival will depend less upon domination of one group of people by another and increasingly upon interdependence, cooperation, and harmony. Historically, however, it has been the patriarchal mind-set that has defined what men are and how they behave as well as what women are and how they behave. In this new age, those stereotypes have been challenged, leading to serious questioning of these age-old definitions. The result has been that sexual patterns based on these definitions are rapidly changing as well. For example, the patriarchally defined marriage began to fail as the divorce rate rose, the double standard of premarital sexual behavior for men and women is falling, the old assumption that all people need to be married to be fulfilled has collapsed, and condemnation of homosexuals has been countered. As these old stereotypes change, sexual behavior will likely change as well.

What brought about all this change? At the time the United States was born, all the stereotypes were still in place. Shortly after the Constitution was signed, women began their long fight for the right to vote. When the Fifteenth Amendment, allowing black men to vote, was passed after the Civil War, women continued the struggle for franchise with renewed vigor. In the 1920s they were successful. A door had opened, and sixty years or so later a woman was nominated for vice president by one of the major political parties. The sexual revolution was upon us.

It should be noted, however, that past sexual patterns had never been quite so clear-cut as contemporary moral traditionalists would have us believe. Even marriage in its beginnings had more of an economic than a moral basis, since it was important to assure that the inheritors of wealth and property were legitimate. Marriage was not demanded by the church until quite recently because the poor had no wealth to protect. In England in the seventeenth century, for example, most marriages were common-law.

Several factors have led to major changes in sexual behaviors. A primary reason has been the lengthening of time between the onset of puberty and the age of matrimony. First, because of improved diet and health, young women now begin their menstrual cycle at age twelve or thirteen instead of at sixteen or seventeen as was common in the eighteenth century. Second, the time required to complete an education has increased because of the higher level of expertise needed for a productive life in modern society. Often, more than ten years now separate marriage from puberty.

There have been other components to these changes as well. Reliable birth control methods reduce the fear of pregnancy that in the past was a deterrent to sexual activity, thus providing sexual freedom for women. Feeding these winds of change are coeducational colleges that do not feel mandated to oversee the private lives of their students, new opportunities for women in the work force, available apartment living for young singles, and improved and accessible transportation. The time of male domination is rapidly coming to a close.

Bishop Spong believes that innovative guidelines and new laws will develop around these changed values. He calls the church in this time of transition to be with its people as they seek new behavior patterns that will be life-enhancing.

BIBLICAL READING

Genesis 38:1–11

NEW INSIGHTS

....

....

....

QUESTIONS FOR REFLECTION

1. Do you agree with the author's assertion that "the patriarchal mentality is almost inevitably homophobic . . . " (p. 42)? Why or why not?

2. Read Ephesians 5:22–33. Comment on these verses in light of the chapter you have just read.

3. In your experience, are there factors other than those mentioned by Spong that explain the sexual revolution?

4. Have you ever heard someone say, "In the past it was so much easier to live—we knew exactly what was right and wrong; there were no gray areas"?

If you are a woman, would you have preferred to live in the eighteenth century with its clear rules and confines of sexual behavior, or in the late twentieth century with all its uncertainties about appropriate behavior? Why? Do you believe a man would respond differently? Why?

If you are a man, would you have preferred to live in the eighteenth century with the sexual certainties of appropriateness or in the twentieth century with its multitude of gray areas? Why? How do you think a woman would respond to the same question? How do you think a woman would expect you to answer?

5. Give examples of what happened to people who broke the traditional morality expectations of the past. In answering this question, use books or films as well as knowledge from your own life or from the lives of acquaintances.

6. Write a short letter to the seminary dean cited on page 47 who wrote that any attempt to rethink ethics, or to change the paternal nature of God, or to surrender the exclusive claim that one small group possesses the only truth, must be "countered at every level."

ACTIVITY

Write again in your journal. Enter your feelings about this chapter as well as any points or issues that you would have liked to discuss with the author.

CHAPTER FOUR

DIVORCE: NOT ALWAYS EVIL

SUMMARY

Traditional marriage in a patriarchal society is based on a dominant-subordinate relationship. Anything that causes a breakdown of the patriarchal society (such as the power shift between the sexes noted in chapter 3) will inevitably cause changes in those institutions—such as marriage—that are shaped by it.

In the nineteenth century the ovum was seen for the first time under a microscope. The result was a visual demonstration that the woman is an equal partner in the reproductive process. For years it had been believed—with a distinctly male bias—that the woman was merely a womb, in which a baby grew as a result of the male's sperm: she added nothing but a warm incubator for that sperm. Thus, when a woman failed to produce a child, it meant *she* was inadequate.

Traditional wedding ceremonies in those patriarchal days included both a question from the clergyman, "Who gives this woman to be married to this man?" and a promise from the woman to "love, honor, and obey" her new husband. At the conclusion of the ritual, the newly married couple was pronounced "man and wife." Thus, one man gave another man "this woman" who promised to "obey" him, and the couple was then presented to the witnesses as "man and wife" rather than "husband and wife." The ceremony itself clearly represented an arrangement for a kept woman. And, indeed, she was. Marriage was a woman's security, since she had no political or economic power. No matter how intolerable a marriage was, divorce was usually worse.

Divorce, when it did occur, presented the woman with a multitude of problems. An arrangement of alimony was devised to address the economic unfairness of the patriarchal system. However, alimony was not always provided and settlements were not always enforced. In any event, the woman was still "kept." Further, capital usually remained with the husband, and a dearth of available jobs impeded the single woman's quest for economic security. Thus, divorce was to be avoided at all costs. If there was a divorce, it was usually initiated by the husband.

World War II was a big turning point for women. As men entered the armed forces, the job market opened for women. It became patriotic for women to work, and they could be seen in heavy industrial and maintenance positions as well as at offices. When the war ended and the men returned, often to attend college, women demanded to be allowed to continue their educations as well, thus increasing job opportunities for women at all levels and in all professions. Obligatory economic dependence for women, *as a class*, had ended.

When marriage ceases to be based on economic dependence and when equal earning potential exists between the sexes, a marriage of peers becomes possible. The old patriarchal model based on power relationships between two unequal persons disappears. In a partnership of equals, however, working together becomes more prone to open conflict. Now that *both* men and women can feel free to divorce, the possibility of divorce is doubled.

The church has traditionally regarded divorce with contempt. In fact, it is the only sin incorporated into official canon law with automatic excommunication for a divorced and remarried person. Yet, despite objection and criticism from official voices of religious institutions, divorce has become commonplace. The author believes that after working to support a marriage, the church should be clear that it does not condemn the individuals involved: a divorce may lead to abundant new life for both persons.

Options for women in this emerging society have multiplied. She may opt for a career with no marriage, or no children even though married. She may choose to be a single parent. This variety of possibilities leads to questions concerning other relationships in which there exists the possibility of sexual love without a commitment of marriage. The moral issues of such decisions need to be addressed. For instance, is sex outside of marriage always sinful? Bishop Spong calls for the church to be present and assisting in the struggle for integrity and meaning within this world of transition.

NEW INSIGHTS

....

....

....

QUESTIONS FOR REFLECTION

1. List from your personal experience or from observations five to ten ways in which marriage has become more of an institution of equals than one built on the former master-servant relationship.

2. Read Mark 10:2–9. Comment on this passage in light of your reading of chapter 4.

3. The pastor of your church has just preached a sermon on the evils of divorce. You are divorced. What would you include in a letter you intend to write to him?

4. Bishop Spong raises a number of questions on page 65. Respond to two of the following three:

"Does the group of people for whom marriage is an asset have a right to impose the standard that enhances their lives upon those people who have chosen a different path?"

"Is sex outside marriage always sinful? What happens when we apply the biblical standard of judging the tree by its fruit? Suppose the manifestations of a committed but unmarried relationship are love, joy, and peace, while bitterness, pain, and hurt are the products of a legal marriage?"

"Can traditional morality be adapted so that the good things it sought to ensure with its particular prohibitions and affirmations might still be accomplished inside a new set of affirmations and prohibitions that are appropriate to the contemporary values . . . ?"

5. Some people claim that the increase in divorce is evidence that marriage vows are being taken less seriously than in the past. Do you agree? Why or why not?

ACTIVITY

Return to your journal and take this opportunity to write your reactions to the material you have just finished. Have you any disagreements with Bishop Spong's statements? Are there any points you feel he omitted? Include these ideas as you write.

CHAPTER FIVE

HOMOSEXUALITY: A PART OF LIFE, NOT A CURSE

SUMMARY

Another element in the changing sexual picture of the last several decades has been an increased awareness of the homosexual person as an integral part of society. Perhaps as much as 10 percent of the population has a homosexual orientation. Many of these men and women have emerged from the silence in which they previously lived to demand the same acceptance and rights as those of the heterosexual community.

Homosexuality was classified as a mental illness until 1973, when it was officially reclassified by the American Psychiatric Association. The seeds of the illness theory came from the work of Sigmund Freud, who believed that homosexuality was caused by a developmental aberration, thus suggesting the hope of a cure. But no cure was found and no conclusive evidence was forthcoming to support this hypothesis. Another explanation proposed by some people has been that homosexuality is a deliberately chosen perversion. These persons then conclude that this "unnatural" behavior is sinful and depraved.

A substantial body of research indicates that homosexuality may be neither a matter of choice nor of environmental factors. Rather, it may be a result of fetal development of the brain. Research is still continuing in this area, but a neurobiological or neurochemical explanation seems likely.

Spong cites many accounts of research in the past two decades on which he bases his conclusion that homosexuality is an unchosen, unchangeable sexual orientation of a significant proportion of the population and constitutes a normal but minority expression of human sexuality.

Some fear that by accepting Spong's conclusions, one is led to an approval of all manifestations of sexual behavior. But it is the moral absolute that proclaims all homosexuality as evil and all heterosexuality as good to which he objects. Destructive, exploitive sexual behaviors are certainly present in both homosexual and heterosexual relationships, and when they occur it should be labeled as the evil it is. Distinctions should be made between life-giving and life-destroying sexual behavior for *all* people, regardless of orientation.

Acceptance of gays and lesbians in society has increased in the past generation. The churches have moved to open dialogue on this long-ignored issue; they are passing resolutions declaring the need for justice for *all* people, and they are responding to persecution of homosexuals by declaring the need for a guarantee of civil rights. Unfortunately, the distinction between orientation and behavior is still often noted. That is, although an individual cannot choose orientation, he or she can choose a lifestyle. In many cases, therefore, homosexuals are told not to act on their homosexual orientation because it is evil. This attitude would have them remain celibate in exchange for the church's blessing on them and their relationships.

It is only when society is able to regard both homosexual and heterosexual orientation as neutral—neither good nor evil per se—that we can move forward on the question of how all people can lead a responsible and life-enhancing sexual life.

Spong believes the church has a major role in this continuing progress. First, it needs to admit to the wrongs of the past and the lack of support for homosexuals. Second, it needs to rethink the ethics of human sexuality, including how it should respond to the many gays and lesbians seeking ordination. Spong's belief that homosexuals should be considered for ordination without regard to their sexual orientation, however, places him in a minority position in his own denomination.

BIBLICAL READING

John 10:10

NEW INSIGHTS

....

....

....

QUESTIONS FOR REFLECTION

1. Complete the sentence "I am _____." Repeat this exercise ten times with ten different answers. Circle the five statements that you feel are most important in determining who you are. Have you included a statement that describes your sexuality? Why or why not? If you did not, what persons do you believe might have included one? Why?

2. Why do you believe Spong has included John 10:10 in this chapter?

3. Some researchers question the 10 percent figure quoted by Spong, suggesting that it is much too high. Do you think it would make any difference if the percentage of homosexuals in the population were only 7 percent or 5 percent or 3 percent?

4. What do you think Spong means when he says that there is nothing unnatural about any shared love, even between two people of the same gender, if that experience calls both partners into a fuller state of being?

5. How would you define the terms *life-giving* and *life-destroying* as they are used in this chapter?

6. Spong has not mentioned bisexuality in this chapter. However, the 1948–53 Kinsey Report suggested that bisexuality was more common than homosexuality. How do you think Spong would respond to this phenomenon?

ACTIVITY

You have now completed the first section of *Living in Sin?* Again enter in your journal the feelings you had after reading this chapter. Add any questions or comments that you would like Bishop Spong to address if he were available.

PART II

The Bible

AN AMBIGUOUS SYMBOL OF AUTHORITY

and

THE CASE AGAINST LITERALISM

(pages 94–106)

SUMMARY

The Bible has long been used as a symbol of authority by those who wish to substantiate their personal views of history, society, ethics, or the world to come. To be able to assert that the Bible is on one's side is to be able to claim obvious correctness. There is such power in quoting the "inerrant word of God," such comfort for those who seek sure and absolute answers. It is not just traditionalists, however, who use the Bible in this way. Those who seek change also find their answers and their support in these holy Scriptures. Historically, both sides on most major societal issues can be found claiming support from the Bible. Witness the defenders as well as the opponents of slavery and the divine right of kings.

Thus, it is not surprising to discover that as society wrestles with changes in sexual behavior in this new age, conservatives and liberals alike quote from the Bible. In the current debates, however, the liberals have been secularized; that is, those calling for a new look at sexual ethics are often people who have left religious institutions, finding them out of touch with the sexual morality of the twentieth century. The conservative side continues to claim a literal understanding of the Bible—becoming ever more hostile as the debate rages. Spong wishes to free the Scriptures from this literalistic prison.

The bishop's own story is one of great love of the Bible, a love that moved from a literal, unquestioning understanding of its stories to a studied exploration of biblical scholarship. His faith, he claims, has been strengthened by this study and research.

It is important to remember that the first of the material that was to become the Hebrew Scriptures was written during the early years of King

Solomon's reign (in the tenth century B.C.E.), some nine hundred years after Abraham lived. Thus, much of our biblical story was transmitted orally for probably twenty-five or more generations before being written.

In addition, many biblical scholars believe that the Hebrew Scriptures represent a weaving of four major strands of tradition into a single whole. The first of these strands is a narrative that has been called the Yahwist tradition from its reference to God as Yahweh. This strand was a court history (written in the southern kingdom of Judah with its capital, Jerusalem, home of King David) to advance the interests of the royal tradition. It portrays God as speaking only with the leaders of the divinely chosen. Yahweh did not communicate directly with the people but through Moses. When the Yahwist writers recorded the narrative, they stressed that rebelling against God's chosen leaders was synonymous with rebelling against God.

A second strand of the story is the Elohist document, so designated because it refers to God by the name Elohim. Dated 850–750 B.C.E., approximately one to two hundred years later than the older Yahwist material, it was the sacred story of the northern kingdom and its capital of Samaria. The northern and southern kingdoms had separated when King Rehoboam, grandson of King David, refused to submit to demands by the military leader Jeroboam. The northern kingdom's traditions differed from those of the south. There was no divinely selected royal family, but rather a king who was chosen by his subjects and could, therefore, be overthrown. When the northern kingdom's historians recalled the experience of Mount Sinai, they remembered a covenant made by God with a whole nation, not just with the divinely chosen leaders of that nation.

When an Assyrian army defeated the northern kingdom in 721 B.C.E., a few persons fled to the south, taking with them their sacred narrative. In time, this history was merged with the Yahwist writings of the south into a single new document. This blending helps to explain many of the inconsistencies that appear in the telling of early Hebrew history.

Strand three was incorporated into the Yahwist-Elohist blended document when a new book of the Law was found within the walls of the temple at Jerusalem in 621 B.C.E. The new material was called the second law, and the claim was made that it had been written by Moses. This new addition is seen primarily in the book of Deuteronomy; historically, it resulted in the centralizing of authority in the priesthood of Jerusalem.

The fourth strand of this biblical heritage appears as a result of the exile experience. To ensure that the Hebrews retained their Jewishness in a foreign land, the priests demanded strict observance of the law and cultic practices. The Jews were to be a people set apart with mandatory circumcision, strict dietary regulations, and rigidly enforced rituals and laws. It was during this period, perhaps the sixth century B.C.E., that priestly writers took the earlier blended document and revised it to satisfy their own theological views. For instance, a new creation story was added to emphasize the day of rest, and the wilderness story was recast so that Moses did not violate the Sabbath.

It is essential for readers to recognize that the biblical text evolved over many years, with many authors, each with his own motivations. A particular verse or portion cannot in conscience be lifted out to defend or disparage an argument that the authors surely never intended or considered.

BIBLICAL READINGS

Genesis 12

Genesis 32

Numbers 12

Romans 13

Genesis 37

Exodus 20

Exodus 34

II Kings 22

Deuteronomy 5

Genesis 7

Exodus 16

I Kings 1

I Chronicles 28–29

NEW INSIGHTS

....

....

....

QUESTIONS FOR REFLECTION

1. Name the four major strands of the Hebrew Scriptures that biblical scholars have identified. In which of these are the seeds of the "priesthood of all believers"? Would our understanding of the ancient Hebrews be better served if we had only the Elohist tradition? The Yahwist tradition? Why or why not?

2. Read both creation stories (Genesis 1–2:3 is the priestly tradition and Genesis 2:4–25 is the older tradition). How do they differ? Which one is more familiar to you? If you already knew there were two tellings of the same story, how did you harmonize their differences in your mind?

3. Which of the three traditions of the Ten Commandments is most familiar to you (Exodus 20, the Elohist tradition; Exodus 34, the Yahwist tradition; or Deuteronomy 5, the deuteronomic tradition)? Did you know there were three distinct versions?

ACTIVITY

Return to your journal and add your observations and feelings after reading chapter 6 and the first portion of chapter 7. Is there anything that confuses you? Are there questions you feel Bishop Spong left unanswered?

THE CASE AGAINST LITERALISM

(pages 106–16)

SUMMARY

The New Testament, like the Hebrew Scriptures, should be analyzed in light of recent biblical scholarship. In looking at the Gospel narratives, scholars believe that Mark was the earliest document and may have been written as a whole. However, Matthew and Luke, written later than Mark, were put together from several different identifiable sources. Matthew, for instance, takes its material from the writings of Mark, a hypothesized Q document (which stands for material common to both Matthew and Luke), and source material available only to the author of Matthew. Luke also uses Mark and either the Q source or Matthew himself, but adds material known only to the author of Luke.

Paul lived and wrote before the appearance of any of the Gospel accounts. His works are the earliest of the New Testament writings, probably dating between 49 and 62 C.E. Some of the epistles attributed to Paul by the early Christian church were most likely written by others. He proclaimed in his writings that God was present in the person of Jesus, and was designated God's Son at the moment of his resurrection (Rom. 1:4).

Mark, writing between 65–70 C.E., suggests that God entered Jesus at his baptism. And yet, twenty to twenty-five years later, when Matthew and Luke were written, the moment of God's entrance into the person of Jesus was placed at the time of conception. Thus, while Mark begins his story with the baptism of Jesus and has no birth narrative, both Matthew and Luke, writing more than fifty years after the death of Jesus, have added this feature to their story. Later yet, when the Gospel of John was written—approximately at the turn of the century—the moment of God and Jesus becoming one is pushed back to the beginning of time. That Gospel therefore begins, "In the beginning was the Word, and the Word was with

God, and the Word was God. He was in the beginning with God. . . . And the Word became flesh and lived among us."

Besides this developing theological concept about Jesus and his identification with God, there are many other inconsistencies among the Gospel narratives. For instance, Mark notes that those who had seen the miracles of Jesus were urged to keep silent so as not to reveal his identity prematurely, while John has a Christ who often and openly asserts, "I am the bread of life" and "The Father and I are One." Further, the details of the resurrection account vary considerably among the Gospels—from the simple account in Mark to the spectacular events, including earthquakes and angels, recorded by Matthew. And anyone who reads the two birth stories in Matthew and Luke will be struck by the considerable differences between them.

It is difficult to believe that, with these many obvious inconsistencies, some persons still claim an absolute inerrancy for this text. Once the case for literalism is set aside, however, there are important questions to ask. Why would this account be preserved? What was the question it answered or the agenda it served? And what are the author's assumptions? Sometimes even the most unambiguous "Thou shalt not" statements have beneath them a level of understanding not considered by the reader. The Ten Commandments, for instance, seem straightforward. Yet on closer examination, murder is forbidden for a Jew against Jew, but is acceptable for a Jew against the Hebrews' enemies.

For centuries, claims Spong, the Bible has been inappropriately quoted by people with their own personal agendas.

BIBLICAL READINGS

2 Timothy 3:16
2 Corinthians 5:19
Romans 1:4
Matthew 1–2
Luke 1–2
John 1:1, 14

Matthew 5:27–28
Exodus 5:1ff.
Exodus 12:36
Exodus 14:30
Deuteronomy 14:21

NEW INSIGHTS

....

....

....

QUESTIONS FOR REFLECTION

1. List the similarities and differences in the two birth stories as presented in Matthew 1–2 and Luke 1–2. Which story is more familiar to you? How do you reconcile their differences?

2. Construct an abbreviated time line showing the following people and events: Abraham; King David and the Yahwist writers; the addition of the Elohist writings to the Yahwist tradition; the deuteronomic and priestly additions to the Hebrew Scriptures; the Gospel writers; and the Pauline writings. What insights does this time line contribute to your understanding of the Bible?

3. Do you think we should give greater credence to those authors or writings that were produced closer in time to the events they recall? For instance, Mark's rather than John's resurrection story? Or Paul's rather than Mark's understanding of when Jesus became One with God? Please explain your answer.

4. Read the resurrection stories in Matthew 28, Mark 16, Luke 24:1–12, and John 20:1–18. Which is the most familiar to you? Do you have any problem with their discrepancies? How have you accommodated these differences in your own thinking?

5. Do you agree with Spong that when details are in opposition, proponents of the two sides of the contradiction cannot both be right? Why or why not?

6. Do you believe there is ever an appropriate time to use the method of proof-texting of the Bible? Explain.

ACTIVITY

Imagine that the author is sitting in your living room. Tell him (by writing in your journal) how you felt after reading this section of his book. Include in your conversation with him either the points on which you disagreed with him or those that you think would have strengthened his case.

CHAPTER EIGHT

THE BIBLICAL ATTITUDE TOWARD WOMEN

SUMMARY

The fact that the Bible has a strong bias against women can be understood by recalling some of the cultural contexts within which it developed. The Hebrew Scriptures were related and later written by worshipers of Yahweh who wished to convey the great events in their history. These events were understood in light of Yahweh's intervention in their corporate life: the plagues in Egypt, the crossing of the Red Sea, the manna in the wilderness, the fall of Jericho. Despite this special relationship with Yahweh, the Hebrew people were attracted by the popular religion of their neighbors—the Baal or idol worship—succumbing over and over to its temptation and falling under its spell.

Baal, with his female and equal consort Asherah, presided over a nature religion that was associated with fertility and the seasons. Yahweh, however, was a solitary male who created life by his Spirit and for whom no female was needed as co-creator. In time, but with much "backsliding," the worship of Baal was successfully supplanted with the worship of a God who presented a distinctly male bias.

The earliest deity worship, according to anthropologists, was probably worship of a goddess representing earth and soil, the mother of all things living. Because woman was the source of life, it was logical to assume that God was female. As the religious thought developed, a male was added as complement to the female deity to provide the necessary rains for new creation, and as a duo they celebrated life. In time, humankind moved from identification with nature and soil to an existence separate from nature and soil and eventually to the conquering of nature. Survival became less dependent on female reproduction than on the male's ability to control nature to meet his needs. Thus the status of the female and female deity declined as the male and male God took their places.

The God of the creation stories in the Bible is understood not as a father but as a king, with no need to share status with a mother. This God stood outside of nature and created it, making man not from a woman but from the earth. Man was called to have dominion over nature. Moreover, since God was a male, only a human male could model this God, and eventually women were relegated to the home with a life that became more limited as male responsibilities grew. In fact, the women were eventually considered possessions of the males.

Throughout the Bible it is possible to see an antifemale bias.

1. The covenant between God and the Hebrew people was a promise between a male God and the Hebrew men. Women related to this God only so long as they were in relationship with men.

2. The law given to Moses on Mount Sinai was directed to men.

3. Man had absolute power over a woman's life and body.

4. The inability of a woman to bear children was her fault and her shame.

5. Adultery was an act that violated another man's *property*.

6. A woman was forbidden to inherit property or to enter into contracts.

The New Testament provides additional examples of this antifemale bias. Paul makes prohibitions against women speaking in church; the author of the letter to Timothy notes that he permits no woman to teach or have authority over men; and the author of the book of Ephesians declares that wives should submit to their husbands.

Some women, especially in the Hebrew Scriptures, do manage to cast off the mantle of submissiveness. Miriam, Deborah, Ruth, Esther, and Judith are all examples of such persons. With few exceptions, however, the roles attributed to men and women in the Bible are those assigned by a patriarchal society to accommodate that society. Spong asks, "What does it mean, in the midst of a sexual revolution, when people call on the church and world to return to the sexual morality of the Bible?" (p. 133). He contends that we must reject a literalistic interpretation and look for the real meaning, the Spirit within the Bible.

BIBLICAL READINGS

I Kings 18:40

II Samuel 11:1

Genesis 1:16

Psalms 74:12–17

Psalms 89:9–12

Job 26:12–13

Isaiah 51:9–10

Exodus 20

Genesis 12

Genesis 20

Genesis 26

Genesis 16

I Samuel 1

Judges 13

Judges 16

Numbers 5

Numbers 36

Numbers 30

Deuteronomy 25

Deuteronomy 22:22

John 8:1–11

Genesis 38

Judges 19

I Corinthians 11:7–9

I Corinthians 14:34ff.

I Timothy 2:11–12

I Timothy 2:15

Ephesians 5:23

Exodus 2

Numbers 12

Judges 4

Ruth 4:18–22

Esther 1–10

NEW INSIGHTS

....

....

....

QUESTIONS FOR REFLECTION

1. Take one minute to write all the words you think of when you hear the word *man*. Repeat this exercise using the word *woman*. Compare your lists. Do you find any surprises? Any stereotypes? Any insights?

2. What are your mental images of God? How do you believe these were shaped?

3. Read Genesis 1:27. What does it mean to be created in the image of God?

4. Spong mentions three components of ancient cities that enforced male dominance. What were they? Are you able to name any similar institutions in modern society that encourage or enforce male dominance?

5. How would you answer Bishop Spong's question, "Do we desire to hold up the biblical image of dominance and submission as the Christian model for male-female relationships in our time?" (p. 133)?

6. Can you imagine the Bible without the male bias that Spong describes? How would it be different? What difference would it make to your faith?

ACTIVITY

You are now ready to add to your journal any impressions, comments, or confusion that arose while you read this chapter and answered the questions for reflection. Include a list of adjectives that describe your feelings.

CHAPTER NINE

THE BIBLE AND HOMOSEXUALITY

SUMMARY

References to homosexuality in the Bible are relatively few compared with references to the sin of idolatry, for instance, and none of the four Gospels mentions it at all. Yet there are several verses or sections that historically have been used by biblical literalists to condemn homosexual activities. Spong examines these passages in some detail to discover their origins and meanings.

The story of Sodom and Gomorrah in Genesis describes events in the life of Lot, the nephew of Abraham. Lot's two guests are threatened by the men of Sodom and, in an act of Middle Eastern hospitality, he protects his visitors—aliens in the city—by offering his two virgin daughters to the mob instead. The story continues with a tale of incestuous activities between Lot and his daughters, activities that produce two sons, Moab and Ammon. The Sodom and Gomorrah story has been used by some people to prove biblical condemnation of homosexual activities. Ignored by these same people, however, is the apparent approval in this passage of gang rape, incest, and the denigration of women. In a similar narrative in Judges, a citizen of Gibeah gives hospitality to an alien and refuses to allow the men of the community to sexually abuse his guest. He offers his own daughter or his guest's concubine to the crowd instead.

The Holiness Code in the book of Leviticus does specifically and apparently unequivocally condemn male homosexual behavior. Israel believed that it was called by God to be a unique people. Perhaps homosexuality was condemned because semen was "wasted" and thus their call "to be fruitful and multiply" was not being accomplished.

Other prohibitions or "truths" from the Scriptures, many from the same Holiness Code, have been rejected because new information and understandings have made them obsolete. The fear of menstruating women, the rejection of those who have a "blemish" (that is, a physical abnormality), the execution of persons who curse their mothers or fathers, all have been abandoned. Spong suggests that individuals are willing to accept one particular prohibition over another because it confirms their particular prejudice.

In the book of Romans in the New Testament, Paul appears to condemn homosexuality. Yet a closer reading of this passage seems to suggest that homosexuality was not the sin, but the punishment. It was faithlessness that was the sin. In 1 Corinthians, Paul includes several lists of people who would not inherit the kingdom. They included robbers, the greedy, drunkards, and sexual perverts. It does appear that Paul would not condone homosexual behavior, but Paul writes from a great sense of his own unworthiness and inner conflict. It is easy to believe, claims Spong, that Paul's personal torment could perhaps have involved his own sexuality. Certainly, the church has abandoned other assumptions held by Paul: that God gave the Jews a spirit of stupor, that Christians should not challenge their governments, that women should be veiled.

The book of 1 Timothy includes kidnappers and immoral persons in a list of people who need to hear the law. By looking at the original Greek from which this passage was translated, however, a case could be made for understanding the text not as a reference to homosexual persons generally, but as a condemnation of the specific situation in which a person kidnaps (enslaves) young boys for sexual exploitation.

The last of the New Testament references to homosexuality are from Jude and 2 Peter. Both of these epistles use Sodom and Gomorrah as examples of those who receive the wrath of God for immorality. Written much later in the life of the new church, a reference to Sodom certainly meant "hellfire" for those who disobeyed the teachings of the church.

Spong asserts that Christians need to be willing to relinquish their old prejudices as new knowledge becomes available.

BIBLICAL READINGS

Genesis 19:1–11

Genesis 18

Genesis 4:1

Genesis 19:14

Genesis 19:26

Judges 19

Deuteronomy 23:17

Leviticus 18:22

Leviticus 20:13

Leviticus 11:44–45

Leviticus 20:26

Genesis 1:28

Leviticus 20:18

Leviticus 21:17

Leviticus 21:18–20

Leviticus 24:14

Leviticus 24:16

Deuteronomy 13:5

Deuteronomy 17:1–8

Leviticus 20:9

Romans 1:26–27

Romans 15:22–24

Romans 1:20ff.

Romans 9–11

Romans 11:24

I Corinthians 6:9–11

I Corinthians 5:10

I Corinthians 5:11

Romans 7:15, 18, 24

II Corinthians 12:7–9

Romans 11:8

Romans 13:1–2

I Corinthians 11:5–16

I Timothy

Jude

II Peter

NEW INSIGHTS

....

....

....

QUESTIONS FOR REFLECTION

1. What is a Marcionite (p. 147)? Do you agree with the Marcionites'
understanding of the place of the Hebrew Scriptures in the Bible?
Why or why not?

2. After reading Genesis 19, do you agree with Spong that the sin of Sodom was the citizens' unwillingness to observe laws of hospitality rather than their desire to indulge in homosexual activity?

3. How would you answer the question posed by Spong on page 142, "Is it right for anyone to suggest that the condemnation of homosexual gang rape is to be equated with the condemnation of homosexuality per se?"

4. What is it that allows many people to attribute to premodern Semites a universal wisdom and assume that their written words are free of ignorance, superstition, or prejudice?

5. What were your thoughts as you read the description of a conflicted and tormented Paul on page 151? Might you come to the conclusion that this had something to do with his views on sexuality? Why or why not?

ACTIVITY

The issue of homosexuality is highly debated in religious circles. Return to your journal and add your feelings after having read this chapter on the Bible and homosexuality. Have you changed your opinions? Have your views been reinforced? Would you argue with Spong about his stances and/or statements? Articulate your impressions in your journal.

CHAPTER TEN

THROUGH THE WORDS TO THE WORD

SUMMARY

Bishop Spong asserts that the prejudiced judgments of a Bible considered inerrant cannot endure. By this he does not mean that the Bible has nothing to say to the contemporary issue of sexual ethics. He suggests instead that if the Bible is to be taken seriously regarding the issues of our time, it cannot be taken literally. The task of a Christian is to seek the Word of God from within these writings.

For example, the Word can be found in the story of creation. It is from this story that we learn of the goodness of creation, and the call for all persons to live in God's presence and image. Such understanding can lead to the revelation that all men and women are of value and none is to be exploited or persecuted. It can also encourage the destruction of barriers created by human beings to protect their nation, their tribe, their parochialism, their prejudice—barriers designed to keep them secure by keeping others out. Unfortunately, it often takes tragedies or disasters for us to discern that the human family is one, sharing a common destiny given in the goodness of creation.

The Word can also be found in the personage of Jesus. In his life can be seen God's love. He embraced all humanity, even those much despised, rejected, or condemned in the culture in which he lived. Many stories in the Gospels reveal his acceptance of beggars, thieves, prostitutes, and the weak. This is the Word as opposed to all the contradictory details of his life that permeate the Gospels. That Word asserts that we are valued no matter what the world around us claims. Finally, the Word was in Jesus because he had the courage to be all that God created him to be. This Word is, therefore, a call for each of us to be all we are created to be.

The Word can also be seen in the Spirit who calls us into community, an experience of unity that does not require conformity. For example, the Pentecost narrative in Acts reveals the Spirit descending on a discouraged and scattered band of disciples, igniting them into heroic undertakings. Through their new spirit-filled life and leadership, a Church was born and flourished.

As a Christian people, we have traveled on a religious journey that has moved us from fertility cults, to tribal deities with covenant and law, to individualism, to an understanding of connectedness. The sexual values in this new age must be based on an understanding of where we have been as well as the knowledge of life as we understand it today. Thus, we must not be bound by the literal word of God based only on the wisdom of yesteryear, but must be free to find the eternal Word of God that will surely encourage us to change and grow, seeking and finding new possibilities in the world in which we live.

BIBLICAL READINGS

Genesis 9:20ff.
Leviticus 25:44ff.
Philemon
Colossians 4:1
Ephesians 6:5ff.
Isaiah 40:4, 5
Genesis 1:31
Luke 2
Matthew 2:9–10
Luke 2:21–39
Luke 2:39
Matthew 2:20–23
Luke 3:23
Matthew 1:16
Mark 10:46ff.
Mark 14:3ff.
Luke 23:32ff.
Luke 17:11ff.
Mark 1:32ff.
John 21:15ff.
Mark 10:35ff.
Acts 12:2
John 21:24
John 6:8ff.
Luke 19:1ff.
Matthew 9:9
Mark 15:21
John 4:7ff.
Mark 10:17ff.
Genesis 1:2
Ezekiel 37:1ff.
Luke 1:35
Acts 2:1ff.

NEW INSIGHTS

....

....

....

QUESTIONS FOR REFLECTION

1. What does Spong mean in this chapter when he uses the phrase *Word of God?*

2. What was the Scopes trial in 1925? Why did the author include a reference to it?

3. Name at least six things that you believe the Bible *as a whole* teaches Christians today.

4. How would you respond to a friend who stated, "It would be so much easier if the church had a list of dos and don'ts that we could refer to and that we knew were changeless"?

5. On page 158, Spong gives several examples of disasters that have led people out of isolation into a recognition that the human family is indivisible, sharing a common destiny, a common danger, and a common hope. Can you name any recent incidents or events that validate this for you?

6. What do you believe the author means when he says, "There are no changeless, eternal creeds or Bibles. There is only the changeless, eternal truth of God" (p. 163)?

ACTIVITY

This chapter concludes the section in *Living in Sin?* entitled "The Bible." Do you think that the author has made his case in a convincing way? In a debate, would you prefer to be on his side or on the side of those who would take the Bible more literally? What arguments would you add if you were supporting him? If you were his debate opponent, what issues or questions would you have him address? Respond to these questions in your journal.

PART III

Some New Proposals

MARRIAGE AND CELIBACY: THE IDEAL AND AN OPTION

and

BETROTHAL: AN IDEA WHOSE TIME HAS COME

SUMMARY

Before considering the options of human relationships that he believes fall inside moral behavior, Bishop Spong applauds the two traditional ideals: faithful, monogamous, lifetime marriage and the celibate life as a self-chosen alternative to marriage.

Marriage has never been easy, but it has become especially difficult in this generation, which faces pressures that are radically different from those of only a few decades ago. For instance, the environment in which young adults come to marriage is fraught with sexuality issues that have become more and more public in recent years. Fear of sexual disease, abortion, sexual abuse, and family planning are only a few of the topics that are widely debated. Additionally, previous assumptions about marriage are breaking down and mutuality is replacing the old pattern of a dominant male and a submissive female. With these and the many other pressures of contemporary life, marriage needs intentional and vigorous preparation as well as support by church and society.

The celibate life can serve as an option for some if it is self-chosen. The death of a spouse or the serious illness or incapacity of a spouse may lead individuals to determine that celibacy is the best choice for them, but it may also be chosen before marriage for a variety of reasons. It must be noted that few people will pursue this option, although those who do can live it openly and honestly.

In addition to the ideals of marriage and celibacy, there is a place for the institution of betrothal. This relationship, present in many ancient societies, consists of a serious commitment that is both faithful and public, but not legal and not necessarily for a lifetime. It would be similar to the contemporary engagement but more expansive, including that ambiguous period known as "engaged to be engaged." This union would be open and serious, and would imply mutual responsibility. To celebrate this relationship, a formal liturgical setting could be designed where both persons state openly their intention to live together in faithfulness.

With the lengthening of time between puberty and the completion of education, it is naive to expect that a moral code of the past will survive. Formerly, guilt, encouraged by church theology, and fear of pregnancy held sexual activity in check. That is no longer true. Although most Christian churches still label all sexual behavior outside of marriage as unequivocally evil, most of their flock are not listening. In fact, many young adults believe that it is not sexual activity outside of marriage that is wrong, but rather sexual activity outside of a meaningful relationship that is inappropriate.

Perhaps a betrothal relationship will not last a lifetime, but it is easier to heal the wounds from this separation than from a divorce with its many legal and social complications. Betrothal offers an option other than casual sex, replacing it with a meaningful commitment highlighted by a liturgical ceremony to symbolize its seriousness.

BIBLICAL READING

Matthew 16:18–19

NEW INSIGHTS

....

....

....

QUESTIONS FOR REFLECTION

1. Look at the list of issues on page 168 that have helped thrust human sexuality into the forefront of our consciousness. Expand this

list with issues recently discussed in the news media. Name as many additional topics as you can.

2. Take three minutes to list as many pressures as you can in contemporary life that are not supportive of marriage and families. Take an additional three minutes to list as many conditions or activities as you can that support marriage and families. Which list was easier to compile? Why?

3. Marriage is such an important institution, says Spong, that it should be prepared for with rigor. What do you suppose he means? What would you suggest?

4. Do you agree with Spong that few people can freely choose a celibate life and then live it with integrity? Why or why not?

5. In your mind, how does a betrothal differ from an engagement?

6. Generally, young adults of the present generation do not believe that sex outside of marriage is wrong; however, sex outside of a meaningful relationship is wrong. Do you agree with this conviction? How would you define a "meaningful relationship"?

7. Imagine that you are a parent whose child wants to enter a contract of betrothal. What would your private reaction be? How would you respond to your child?

8. Do you think a liturgical ceremony is necessary for a betrothal? Why or why not? What other options would you suggest?

9. Are there times when sexual attraction is present yet betrothal would not be appropriate because a sustained commitment is missing? How do you believe Spong would deal with that phenomenon?

ACTIVITY

Once again, enter your feelings in your journal. At this point you may have questions you believe the author has not addressed. Note these in your journal, along with any theological, sociological, or historical issues on which you disagree with him.

SHOULD THE CHURCH BLESS DIVORCE?
and
BLESSING GAY AND LESBIAN COMMITMENTS

SUMMARY

Proposed trial liturgies for "A Service for the Recognition of the End of a Marriage" have recently come into existence. A description of a couple participating in such a service gives the reader a sense of the solemnity and pain that accompany it. Close friends of both the man and the woman were present in a church setting similar to the one in which they had taken their original vows. This time, however, they wished to acknowledge publicly and before God that their marriage could no longer continue. Both spoke to the other of the pain of failure and loneliness, each asking the other's forgiveness and pledging to be friends. The gathered congregation affirmed and supported their new promises to each other—of goodwill, caring, and love of their children.

Perhaps this service was unusual. Yet the Church claims that the ultimate purpose for humankind is fullness of life for each of God's creatures. When marriage assists in the fulfilling of that purpose, it is truly beautiful. When a marriage does not support that purpose, however, it can be life-shattering. The church must assert that there are times when divorce is the only alternative that produces hope for life, while remaining in a bad marriage results only in death.

The church must also acknowledge its errors of the past as they relate to the lives of the homosexual men and women in its midst. One way for the church to admit publicly that it has taken part in this sin of oppression is to bless and affirm the love of two people of the same gender who make a mutual commitment to each other. (Note that this is not a marriage ceremony but a blessing. The state defines a legal marriage; the church only confers its blessing.)

Over the years the church has bestowed its blessing on numerous things, including houses, crops, animals, and ships. There is no reason to withhold this blessing from the commitment made by two people for a life that will produce completeness for each of them. Such blessings are already performed by many clergy as a pastoral rite, quietly. But the church of the future should be more open and honest in this practice. Openness will not only allow society to think of these people as a couple rather than as individuals, but it will also announce to the homosexual community that there is an alternative to either celibacy or sexual promiscuity.

BIBLICAL READINGS

Psalm 130
Mark 2:17
Acts 2

NEW INSIGHTS

....

....

....

QUESTIONS FOR REFLECTION

1. Do you believe that a liturgical service such as "A Service for the Recognition of the End of a Marriage" as described by Spong could have been used by any of the divorced people you know? Do you think that there are times when it would be inappropriate? What conditions would make such a service possible or not possible?

2. Do you agree with those who claim that the availability of such a service would encourage divorce? Do you believe that this kind of ceremony would signal an affirmation of divorce by the church?

3. If you were designing such a liturgy, what would you add or change from the one described in chapter 13?

4. Spong compares divorce to a death. Do you agree with this analogy? Why or why not?

5. On page 199, Spong lists instances in which an oppressed people such as the Jews have been productive and creative after throwing off their bondage. What other groups could you add to this example? Do you think there is any difference between ethnic oppression and homosexual prejudice?

6. How would you describe "responsible sexual behavior" for homosexual people? How do you believe this compares with "responsible sexual behavior" for heterosexual people?

7. What would you include in a liturgical service for the blessing of a gay or lesbian commitment?

8. If church blessing of gay and lesbian commitments became part of the liturgy of Christian churches, do you believe it would be more likely that homosexuals would then desire to be ordained as clergy? Would you be concerned about such a move? Why or why not?

9. Name five to ten instances in history where change took place despite the original objection of those in positions of power who decried such change as wrongheaded.

10. Why do you think Spong included Acts 2 in the biblical readings for chapter 14?

ACTIVITY

These two chapters are provocative and will undoubtedly raise many questions for you. In your journal, list the things you would wish Bishop Spong to address.

CHAPTER FIFTEEN

POST-MARRIED SINGLES AND HOLY SEX

SUMMARY

The number of years people spend in singlehood has been increasing. Although there are a number of causes for this, two are primary: divorce and a longer period before marriage owing to both an increased number of people continuing their schooling and the now socially acceptable career option for women. Yet the church continues to accept marriage as the norm and singleness as something less. This attitude is reinforced by prohibitions against homosexual activity, against unmarried sex, and against divorced persons remarrying without submitting to demeaning procedures to obtain permission.

Many post-married or mature single people may not be interested in marriage or remarriage due to economic or emotional deprivation, demands of others on their resources, or careers that require mobility. Yet the need for companionship does not disappear from a single person's life and sexual abstinence should not be expected.

What are the ethical boundaries for a relationship of single people in which sexual activity is present? One Christian church suggested in an early study that "the physical expression of one's sexuality in relation to another ought to be appropriate to the level of loving commitment within the relationship" (p. 215). Commitment requires a willingness to be vulnerable, and the level of that commitment and vulnerability suggests the level of sexual activity that is appropriate.

Sex outside of marriage can be holy if certain guidelines are met: (1) Both people are single. (2) Sexual activity emanates from a loving and caring relationship. (3) Sexual activity grows out of a relationship over time—it does not initiate it. (4) The relationship is private and discreet to safeguard the vulnerability of both partners. (5) The relationship is exclusive. Under these circumstances, sex between single people can be life-enhancing and thus holy.

BIBLICAL READINGS

Genesis 2:25
Genesis 3:5

NEW INSIGHTS

....

....

....

QUESTIONS FOR REFLECTION

1. Explain the word *vulnerability* as it is used in this chapter.

2. What does it mean to say that when sex enhances life, it is good, but when it destroys or diminishes life, it is evil? Do you agree with this as an ethical standard for sexual activity?

3. This chapter is about sexual activity for post-married and mature singles. Do you think the same comments and standards that are suggested for this population are appropriate for teenagers? For college students? For gays and lesbians?

4. On page 216, Spong offers five guidelines to holy sex and suggests that these five probably do not exhaust the list. What others would you add?

5. Do you agree with Spong's statement that a sexual relationship needs to be exclusive? Why or why not?

ACTIVITY

Many people over the years have questioned the church's stance on sexual behavior for mature adults. Write in your journal your feelings after having read this chapter. Do you feel supported, validated, angry?

CHAPTER SIXTEEN

WOMEN IN THE EPISCOPATE: SYMBOL OF A NEW DAY FOR THE CHURCH

NOTE: When Bishop Spong wrote this chapter in 1988, the Episcopal church still had not consecrated a woman bishop. In 1989, however, the Reverend Barbara C. Harris was elected in the Diocese of Massachusetts, and by 1994 two more women had joined her in the House of Bishops.

SUMMARY

The most powerful institution in defining sexual values and ethics in our society has been the Christian church. Yet this dominance was accomplished in an environment where the leadership was overwhelmingly male. The result has been an image of the divine that is male. Moreover, the language of the liturgy is strongly male—and has been since the earliest years of the church. And influenced by the early church writers, the church has idealized a woman who is a virgin while denigrating women in general.

Although women have been ordained recently in most denominations, very few are yet in positions of power. In the Episcopal church, correcting this imbalance will mean bringing an increased presence of women to the episcopate. Only then will debates on abortion and the morality of such birth issues as artificial insemination be carried on in an atmosphere where both genders can bring their insight and experience. Until the past few years, there have been no women to temper the maleness of discussion in the churches of the Anglican communion.

NEW INSIGHTS

....

....

....

QUESTIONS FOR REFLECTION

1. The church is, according to the author, a sexist institution. Can you name other institutions that would fit that description? What do they have in common?

2. On page 220, Spong gives several examples to support his statement that the language of the liturgy is strongly male dominated. Are you able to add to his list? Are you aware of any attempts to change this situation?

3. Read 1 Corinthians 14:34–35 and 1 Timothy 2:12. How would you interpret their meanings for Christians today?

4. Do you believe there are valid reasons for limiting access to the ordained ministry or to the episcopate to males only? What are the advantages and/or disadvantages of having women in leadership positions in the church?

5. Comment on Spong's statement that "there is something unethical about people of one gender determining the fate of the other" (p. 221).

ACTIVITY

In your journal, write your feelings and concerns about this chapter of *Living in Sin?* Are you left with any unanswered questions?

EPILOGUE: ENDURING THE PRESENT TO CLAIM THE FUTURE

SUMMARY

The author hopes for debate on his ideas and proposals. They are written, he asserts, not just to the faithful remnant still in the pews of the Christian churches, but to those who have left as well. He recognizes, however, that people who in the past had threatened the tradition and security of the church and its leadership with pioneering ideas often did not live long enough to see their insights alter the institution. Using as examples Copernicus, Galileo, Darwin, and Bishop Pike, among others, he notes that change often comes slowly. His hope is that this next transformation—the one in which we can encounter honesty about what the Bible is and is not, about what it says about women and sexual behavior and what it does not—will come more rapidly than in the past.

CONCLUSION

You have now completed *Living in Sin? A Bishop Rethinks Human Sexuality*. A few final tasks remain to determine if your objectives in reading this book have been accomplished.

1. Return to the beginning of your Study Guide and look through the "New Insights" you noted from each section or chapter. Do you believe you were led to many new ideas, facts, or understandings by reading this book? Mark those that were most meaningful to you. Did you find as many of these new ideas or discoveries in the biblical readings as you did in the pages of *Living in Sin?* Was this a surprise? As you look at the "New Insights" from the sixteen chapters and compare them, do you notice any patterns or any areas where you might choose to continue reading or to initiate personal research?

2. Look at the first entry in your journal and read the list of goals you noted before you started the book. How many were achieved? What

might have been changed by either you or the author to satisfy more of your expectations?

3. Now spend some time looking through the entries made in your journal as you completed each chapter or section of the book. The purpose of this Study Guide activity was to enable you to articulate your feelings about the highly provocative material the author was presenting. In some cases, it was expected that you might even encounter some of your own biases or prejudices. As you reread these entries, do you find the earlier ones similar to or different from those you wrote later? How would you explain this? What have you learned about yourself? For instance, how do you react to ideas that challenge your values? If you found yourself in a debate on these issues of sexual behavior, biblical literalism, and women in the church, what would be your stance? Do you think reading *Living in Sin?* has changed any of your views? Reinforced them? After having read this book and worked through the accompanying Study Guide, would you recommend it to someone else? Why or why not?

GUIDELINES FOR GROUP STUDY OF

LIVING IN SIN?

The intent of the following section is to assist a leader in designing a six-week course for use with a group of adults interested in reading and discussing *Living in Sin?* The material has been adapted to conform to the traditional one-hour Christian education time schedule available in many churches on Sunday mornings; however, if the group is meeting at another time, it is recommended that seventy-five to ninety minutes be allocated for each session.

PURPOSE OF THE COURSE

Since John Shelby Spong hoped that *Living in Sin?* would elicit dialogue and debate on the controversial issues he raised, this course is designed to have participants

- read and understand the author's major arguments and the supporting biblical passages
- be aware of both new insights they have gained and feelings or biases they carry to any dialogue based on this provocative material
- be able to articulate their own views in either support of or opposition to those presented in the book

These goals are to be accomplished by a multifaceted approach involving short presentations by the leader, small discussion groups, and journal writing. A limited amount of homework is also recommended.

GATHERING THE PARTICIPANTS

Before the first session is scheduled, the leader should bring together those adults who have expressed an interest in participating in a six-week course. Each person should be able to acquire a copy of the book or, alternatively, the leader may arrange to obtain the books for the group. Because the sessions will not be designed as lectures, it is essential that all participants commit themselves to reading the designated material before each class meeting. The leader should also request at this time that each person bring the following items to all class meetings: a notebook that can be used as a personal journal, a New Revised Standard Version of the Bible, and a pen or pencil. The time and date of the first meeting should be announced and the first assignment given. (It is recommended that a schedule of the meeting dates, a list of the necessary materials, and the first assignment all be prepared in advance and distributed at this intro-ductory gathering.)

IDEAS FOR CREATING A HEALTHY GROUP ENVIRONMENT

1. The meeting place should be as comfortable and spacious as pos-sible, allowing participants to meet in both small and large groups.

2. The purpose of each session should be clearly stated and all agen-das and time frames noted. Ideally, this information should be prepared in print and distributed to the participants as they arrive at each class.

3. An environment of trust is essential if all members of the group are to participate in the various discussions in the six meetings. In order for this to occur, individuals should value other members of the group and lis-ten to their views despite the strong possibility that they may find them-selves in disagreement. Each person should be accorded dignity and respect and all opinions treated with seriousness. All group members should have an opportunity to contribute to a discussion, and no one per-son should be allowed to dominate the discussion.

4. Either the leader or a participant assigned to the task should open and close each meeting with an appropriate prayer.

5. The leader or co-leaders should arrive at each session well pre-pared and on time. The meeting room should be inviting and ready, with the necessary materials on hand. The objective of the day's session should be on display in the room—written on either a chalkboard or a flip-chart. All sessions should start and end at the appointed time.

ASSIGNMENT TO BE DISTRIBUTED TO ALL CLASS MEMBERS BEFORE THE FIRST MEETING

1. Read all introductory material and chapters 1–3 of *Living in Sin?*

2. Using the New Revised Standard Version (NRSV) of the Bible, read all biblical passages cited in these three chapters.

3. Divide your journal or notebook into two equal parts. Label the first section "New Insights" and the second section "Feelings, Reactions, and Responses." Note in the "New Insights" portion any new ideas or understandings you have acquired in the assigned reading—both book and Bible.

4. In the second section of the journal, register your feelings about the material you have been reading. It may help to imagine the author sitting across from you in your living room. What would you say? Do you agree with him? Disagree? Are you angry? (Keep in mind that you will not be sharing this portion of the assignment with anyone in the class unless you choose. This is your personal response to the material you are engaging.)

5. Answer the following question: If, as the author claims, the Bible itself is not free of contradictions and expressions of prejudice, of what value is this collection of books Christians call sacred Scripture?

Session 1

OBJECTIVES

- To acquaint class members with the format of the six-week course
- To examine the biblical call to inclusiveness
- To note the changing patterns of male-female relationships
- To begin work with journals

INTRODUCTION AND PRAYER (10 minutes)

1. Open class with a prayer.

2. Indicate objectives for both the complete six-week course and the first session of the course.

3. Write out and display the format that will be followed for this first session, with times inserted.

4. Have group members introduce themselves. Note that they will be working with one another in small, changing groups over the next several weeks.

5. Ask for volunteers for opening and closing prayers for sessions 2 through 6.

PRESENTATION (10 minutes)

Leader summarizes the material in the first three chapters and allows for a short period for questions or comments.

DISCUSSION (20 minutes)

Break the class into small groups of four or fewer people each. Their assignment in these groupings is to discuss the following questions: (1) What new insights or information did you gain in either the home reading or the leader's summary? (2) What was the most problematic or challenging material for you in this section? (3) How would you as a group answer the question you were assigned as homework for this first week? (4) Discuss two reflection questions selected from the Study Guide by the leader.

Each group should prepare a very brief response to each of these questions.

SUMMARY (10 minutes)

Return to the large group and have one person from each subgroup display the answers that his or her group developed. The leader should comment on similarities and differences discerned in the responses.

JOURNAL (5 minutes)

Provide time for participants to add to both sections of the Study Guide and to their journals.

ASSIGNMENT (5 minutes)

Hand out the following assignment for the next session.

1. Read chapters 4 and 5 of *Living in Sin?* and any biblical references that are included.

2. Enter in your journal the new insights that have come to you as a result of your reading. Then, using the section of your journal labeled "Feelings, Reactions, Responses," record your feelings about this material.

3. Complete the sentence "I am _____" ten times, with ten different answers. Circle the five statements that you think are most important in determining who you are.

CLOSING PRAYER

Session 2

OBJECTIVES

■ To explore twentieth-century changes in the institution of marriage
■ To examine recent research on homosexuality and determine what this means for the moral arena

OPENING PRAYER

PRESENTATION (15 minutes)

Leader presents a summary of material in chapters 4 and 5 and allows a short time for questions and comments.

DISCUSSION (25 minutes)

As you did last week, break into groups of no more than four persons each. The membership of these groups should be as different as possible from the previous session. Give them the following assignment, asking them to report briefly on their answers to each question to the larger group. (1) What new information did you discover in these two chapters? (2) In response to the home assignment where you were requested to answer the "I am _____" question, did you include a statement that described your sexuality? Why or why not? If you did not, what persons do you believe might have included one? Why? (3) List from personal experience, or from observations, ways in which marriage has become more of an institution of equals than one built on the former master-servant relationship. (4) How would you describe the terms *life-giving* and *life-destroying* used in chapter 5?

A member of each group should be ready to share the group's comments.

SUMMARY (10 minutes)

Return to the large group and have the groups' representatives display the answers that their groups have developed to the questions. When each group has finished, the leader should comment on areas of agreement or disagreement.

JOURNAL (5 minutes)

Provide five minutes for participants to add to either or both sections of their journal as a result of this session.

ASSIGNMENT (5 minutes)

Hand out the following assignment for the next session.

1. Read chapters 6 and 7 of *Living in Sin?* and *all* biblical references. Note: This will take longer than earlier readings.

2. Write in both sections of your journal as before.

3. Name the inconsistencies in the Scriptures that bother you the most. Are you able to explain why they affect you?

CLOSING PRAYER

Session 3

OBJECTIVES

- To review the historical development of the holy Scriptures
- To become acquainted with some of the inconsistencies in the Bible

OPENING PRAYER

PRESENTATION (15 minutes)

Leader summarizes the material in chapters 6 and 7 and allows sufficient time for comments and questions. During this summary, display a time line to give participants a sense of the historical framework. (See the Questions for Reflection following chapter 7.) Show the following people and events: Abraham; King David and the Yahwist writers; the time at which the Elohist writings were added to the Yahwist tradition; the priestly and deuteronomic additions to the Hebrew Scriptures; the Gospel writers; and the Pauline writers.

DISCUSSION (25 minutes)

Once again, divide the class members into small groups. Each group is to discuss the following four questions: (1) What new data or knowledge did you gain from reading this section of the book? (2) Which inconsistencies in either the Hebrew Scriptures or the New Testament are most unsettling to your group? (3) If you were aware that the birth narratives in Matthew and Luke were so different, how did you accommodate these differences in your mind? (4) Do you think we should give greater credence to those authors or writings that are closest in time to the events they recall? For instance, Mark's rather than John's resurrection story?

Each group should designate one of its members to record a brief response to each of these questions.

SUMMARY (10 minutes)

Return to the large group, where the groups' representatives will display the answers their groups have prepared. When all have completed this task, the leader will respond with observations.

JOURNAL (5 minutes)

Allow a few minutes for participants to add to their journals any new insights or feelings they may have realized during this session.

ASSIGNMENT (5 minutes)

Distribute the following assignment for the next session.

1. Read chapters 8 through 10 of *Living in Sin?* and all biblical references. Note: This is the longest assignment in the six-week course.

2. Write in both sections of the journal.

3. Respond to this question: What were your thoughts as you read on page 151 the description of a conflicted and tormented Paul? Might you come to the conclusion that this had something to do with his views on sexuality? Why or why not?

CLOSING PRAYER

Session 4

OBJECTIVES

- To recognize the antifemale bias in the Bible
- To evaluate the biblical references to homosexuality
- To discover the Word in the Bible

OPENING PRAYER

PRESENTATION (15 minutes)

Leader summarizes the material in chapters 8, 9, and 10, allowing sufficient time for comments and questions.

DISCUSSION (25 minutes)

Divide the class members into small groups, once again trying to place them with people with whom they have not worked before. Each group should answer the following two questions: (1) What new insights have you gained in reading these three chapters? (2) Name five things that you believe the Bible *as a whole* teaches Christians today.

In half the groups, add the following two questions: (3) What are your mental images of God? How do you believe these were shaped? (4) Read Genesis 1:27. What does it mean to be created in the image of God?

In the other groups, add the following questions: (3) Read Genesis 19. Do you agree with Bishop Spong that the sin of Sodom was in the citizens' unwillingness to observe laws of hospitality rather than in their desire to indulge in homosexual activity? (4) How did you answer the homework question about Paul?

Remind each group to appoint one of its members to record a very brief response to each of these questions.

SUMMARY (10 minutes)

Return to the large group and have the groups' representatives display their groups' responses. The leader should be ready to comment as before.

JOURNAL (5 minutes)

Provide time for participants to add to both sections of their journals as a result of this session.

ASSIGNMENT (5 minutes)

Distribute the following assignment for the next session.

1. Read chapters 11 through 13 of *Living in Sin?* and the biblical references.

2. Write in both sections of the journal.

3. Take three minutes to name as many pressures as you can in contemporary life that are *not* supportive of marriage and families. Take an additional three minutes to list as many conditions or activities as you can that support marriage and families. Which list was easier? Why?

CLOSING PRAYER

Session 5

OBJECTIVES

■ To consider the option of betrothal in addition to the options of marriage and celibacy
■ To consider whether the church should bless divorce

OPENING PRAYER

PRESENTATION (15 minutes)

Leader summarizes the material in these three chapters and allows for a short period for questions or comments.

DISCUSSION (25 minutes)

Divide the class into small groups and give them the following assignment: (1) Did you discover any new information in these three chapters? (2) How did members of the group answer the homework question about marriage? (3) In your mind, how is betrothal different from an engagement? (4) It is often said that although young adults of the present generation do not believe that sex outside of marriage is wrong, they do believe that sex outside of a meaningful relationship is wrong. Do you agree? How would you define a meaningful relationship?

A member of each group should be prepared to share his or her group's brief response to each question.

SUMMARY (10 minutes)

Return to the large group and have the groups' representatives display the answers their groups have developed. The leader should comment on similarities or differences in the responses as appropriate.

JOURNAL (5 minutes)

Allow a few minutes for participants to add to their journals as a result of this session.

ASSIGNMENT (5 minutes)

Hand out the following assignment for the next session.

1. Read the remainder of *Living in Sin?* and all biblical references.

2. Write in both sections of the journal.

3. On page 216, Spong details five guidelines to holy sex and suggests that they probably do not exhaust the list. What others would you add?

CLOSING PRAYER

Session 6

OBJECTIVES

- To consider whether the church should bless gay and lesbian commitments
- To examine the possibility of holy sex among older singles
- To evaluate the course

OPENING PRAYER

PRESENTATION (15 minutes)

Leader summarizes the material in chapters 14, 15, and 16, allowing a short period for questions or comments.

DISCUSSION (25 minutes)

Break the class into small groups and have each answer the following questions: (1) How would you describe "responsible sexual behavior" for homosexual people? How do you believe this compares with "responsible sexual behavior" for heterosexual people? (2) Discuss the guidelines for holy sex that you detailed in your home assignment.

A member of each group should be prepared to present his or her group's responses to these questions.

SUMMARY (10 minutes)

Return to the large group and have the groups' representatives share their groups' brief responses to the questions. The leader should be prepared to comment as appropriate.

JOURNAL (10 minutes)

Provide time for class members to reread their journal entries for the past six weeks. Have each person write on a sheet of paper a statement about self-discoveries or knowledge gained as a result of reading *Living in Sin?* The papers are not to be signed, but placed in a box anonymously, so that leaders can later evaluate course success.

CLOSING PRAYER